next level **SOUL** *PRESENTS*

WHISPERS
OF THE
SOUL®

A COLLECTION OF SPIRITUAL POEMS
FOR RELATIONSHIPS

BY CONNIE H. DEUTSCH

LFH
BOOKS

Next Level Soul™ Presents: Whispers of the Soul® A Collection of Spiritual Poems for Relationships

Copyright © 2022 by Connie H. Deutsch

Cover Art & Book Design: IFH Books
Photography by: Aperture Vintage

Next Level Soul™ is a trademark of IFH Industries, Inc.
All Rights Reserved.

IFH Books - A Division of IFH Industries Inc.
13492 N. Highway 183 #120-757
Austin, TX 78750
www.nextlevelsoul.com/books

Ordering Information:
Quantity sales: Special discounts are available on quantity purchases by corporations, associations and others. For details contact the publisher at the address above.

Orders by US trade bookstores and wholesalers:
Please contact the publisher at the address above.

Printed in the United States of America

ISBN Paperback: 979-8-9858940-1-1
First Edition

DEDICATION

Since this is a book about relationships, I'd like to dedicate this book to the people in my life who meant the most to me in the past and the present.

My son, Bruce gave me new meaning in my life. His birth was the most joyous point of my life and remains so to this day. If ever a mother could feel blessed it was having a son like him, a joy to raise and a joy to watch him grow into a man who gives new meaning to the words integrity and honor. I've always loved his curiosity about everything and his love of learning new things. Parents can teach a child many things but children can teach their parents so much more. It's been a pleasure acting as his teacher but I think it's been more of a pleasure letting him teach me. His sense of humor brightens my days and I've never met anyone who didn't love him as soon as they met him. Once again, I feel blessed that he has played such an important part of my life.

My brothers, Michael and Kenny taught me what unconditional love feels like. No matter what I did or didn't do, I knew that they would always love me. That defines for me the meaning of unconditional love, especially when I remember all the times they had to argue about whose turn it was to wake me up in the morning. I was an exceptionally heavy sleeper and always a night owl. When morning came around, I was a miserable person to try to wake up. Every day, I would hear them arguing, "It's your turn to wake her up; I woke her up yesterday." Of course, the other one would reply, "No, you didn't; I woke her up yesterday." They made enough noise about who should wake me up that they could have awakened the dead but I still slept through it. Not too many years ago, my landlord stopped me to ask how I made out in the earthquake and I asked, "What earthquake?" I had slept through it and might not have believed there had been one if I didn't see the garbage cans and lawn chairs scattered all across the lawns of my neighbors. It was a miracle that my house wasn't touched but I'm pretty sure that I would have slept through it anyway.

My parents were my role models. They always emphasized the importance of honesty and integrity and lived by that code of ethics. My mother was love incarnate; I never met anyone who didn't love her and there were hundreds of people who attended her funeral. She had a curiosity about everything and all my friends envied me for having her as my mother. She would ask them the most personal questions that would have me trembling in my boots waiting for her to answer. One day, she asked a man how his wife was and he said that she had committed suicide the day before. When she told me about the encounter she said, "I was so embarrassed; I'll never ask anyone else a personal question again." I smiled and said, "Mom, I'd bet anything that you will continue to ask personal questions of everyone." She shook her head and said no, but an hour later I heard her asking another stranger a deeply personal question. Still, she was loved by everyone,

My father was a different kettle of fish. He was considered charming by everyone but as a daughter, I saw a different side of him. He was a strong disciplinarian and expected perfection from his progeny. I seem to have inherited his perfectionist traits. It took me many years to learn that I didn't have to know all the information in our many encyclopedias or the definition of every word in the many dictionaries in our house. Still, he lived by his own strict code of ethics and taught me the meaning of integrity by his example. He taught me more about health than doctors learn in medical school and almost by osmosis, he laid the groundwork for my future in alternative medicine. He died before he got to see the fruits of his labor since I spent many decades designing health programs for people around the world. I was very fortunate to have had such excellent role models who gave me the stability to be my own person and to think for myself, question everything, and not care about public opinion.

To my brother, Michael, and the love of his life, Michelle Damare, you are an adorable couple, smart, loving, and creative, and I wish you both a long and healthy life. I'm glad you found each other. Just be happy; you deserve the best of everything.

To Alex Ferrari who has always seemed like a member of my family. You were so young when I met you, there were times it felt as though I was raising two children, both extraordinary in their own ways and both very creative, kind, and intelligent. I thank God for the many blessings He has given me and I will try to spend all the days of my life earning those blessings.

- Connie H. Deutsch

TABLE OF CONTENTS

INTRODUCTION

I call these poems my relationship poems because they were the outgrowth of thirty years of doing counseling and a lifetime of studying human nature. People are extremely interesting because of their complexities. Each one possesses his own special set of attributes, idiosyncrasies, foibles, and talents, and each one has a much wider range of potential than he will ever use in one lifetime.

Every time I have ever seen a teacher's comments on a report card saying that the child is not working up to his potential, I smile to myself, thinking, 'neither is the teacher.' I think if we could connect all the untapped potential of every person in a large city, we would probably generate enough energy to light up the world.

Of all the things I've ever done professionally, the aspect of my work that has given me the greatest pleasure is the emotional counseling. There is nothing more exciting to me than exploring the human psyche and seeing what makes people tick.

It's always fascinating to see why five children, born into the same family with the same parents, the same siblings, the same teachers, schools, lifestyle, etc., can each experience life so differently. Why are their personalities, preferences, dislikes, goals, and relationships so different from one another?

There must be much more to it than the birth order. There must be untold and unseen forces at work to make it so.

I think of the mind as resembling the many layers of an onion. To get to the root of one's problems, you have to carefully peel back each layer of the psyche, one layer at a time, so that the person can process the information in a meaningful way and then integrate it into his life. The more layers he strips away, the more control he has over his own life because there are fewer dark corners of his mind that limit his freedom.

This translates into the difference between someone having the ability to act in difficult situations rather than react to them. If he has a clear grasp of a situation and doesn't let his fears rule him, he can act in his own best interests; if he doesn't, then other people will be pushing his buttons and making him react in ways that are not to his liking.

People don't usually change their behavioral patterns unless they are forced to do so, nor do they like to make major changes in their life, particularly of a personal nature. The exception to the rule may be if they have experienced some life-defining moment, losing a loved one unexpectedly, having an accident, being at death's door and getting a second chance, etc., but it has to be severe enough to make them want to change.

It can't be forced on them and they can't do it for someone else; they have to do it for themselves because they want it, not because the other person wants it. They may not rebel against moving halfway across the country, but they may get very upset over being told they have to go on a diet or give up their morning coffee.

Old patterns are the most difficult to break. I often have to remind people that permanent changes don't come quickly or easily; they manifest slowly, through evolution, not revolution. Some people have the mind-set that if this was good enough for their parents, it's good enough for them, or, "I've done this for twenty years and I'm not going to change the way I'm doing it now."

Over the last four decades, I've had the opportunity to meet people from all walks of life and help guide them through their trials and tribulations. Some have been in abusive relationships, some have come from alcoholic parents. Many of them are either very self-absorbed or are in a relationship with a self-absorbed person.

The same can be said of people who think the world owes them a living; either they have entitlement issues of their own, or they are in a relationship with someone who does all the taking and none of the giving. Many of them put up invisible walls and have trouble reaching out and asking for help.

Then there are those who punish others with the silent treatment or have themselves felt the harshness of someone else's wall of silence as a means of punishment. Many people don't want to involve themselves in other people's problems, so they tend to isolate themselves by settling for superficial relationships where neither party feels comfortable enough to ask for help when it is needed. And, not surprisingly, most of them have experienced rejection in one form or another and are too afraid to take emotional risks.

My poems are about these people and the wide array of issues they have had to deal with. Many of these poems focus on the family dynamics, how each one in the household is dealing with a particular problem.

In one of them, we see how each member of the family is being affected by their parents' alcoholism as seen through the eyes of a six-year-old child. In another, we see how secrecy can be viewed as a behavioral disorder when a person doesn't know how to differentiate between what should be kept confidential and what can be shared, so everything becomes a secret.

Several of the poems deal with prevailing attitudes such as are found in the dating scene, the issues of selfishness, entitlement, jealousy, rejection, and the damaging effects of gossip. Then there are a couple of poems that deal with universal problems: the invisible walls that people build to hide behind so they don't get hurt, and the most difficult dilemma of all: knowing when to leave a relationship.

I thank my clients for giving me the opportunity to help them identify their feelings, change their destructive behavior patterns, and heal their souls. I have learned much from them. And most of all, I thank God for giving me the gift of knowing human nature and the ability to guide people into happy, productive lives.

THE FACE IN THE MIRROR

Whose face do you see in the mirror?
Are there character lines that you see?
Do your actions match your reflection
Of the person you want it to be?

When you see your neighbors have problems
Do you offer to lend them a hand?
If they need someone to talk to-
Do you listen? Do you understand?

Do you turn to God in your troubles?
Do you welcome Him into your life?
Do you thank Him for all you've received-
For not only the joy, but the strife?

At the end of the day we are left
With memories of things we have done
There's no one to judge but ourselves
To gauge what we've lost or we've won.

Have you done whatever it takes
To be the very best you can be?
When you see your face in the mirror
Do you like the person you see?

DON'T LET LOVE SLIP AWAY

What emotional risks do you take?
Are your dreams curdling up inside?
Do you tell your loved ones you're hurting?
Or is this the way that you hide?

We waste so many precious moments
Pretending bad things are unseen
A lifetime is spent feeling guilty
For uttering words we don't mean.

We acknowledge our everyday thoughts
Our feelings don't see light of day
When we play by the rules of this game
We lose by the things we don't say.

Our connection to God is the start
Our trust in each other is key
Without intimate moments in life
Our feelings of love cease to be.

We must cherish the moments we have
And express our feelings each day
We don't know what tomorrow will bring;
Hold tight; don't let love slip away.

THE LISTENING HEART

When you listen with your ears
You may hear the sounds of birds
But when you listen with your heart
That's when you will hear their words.

People talk and don't say much
Their words pour out like falling rain.
You must listen with your heart
If you want to hear their pain.

Words are good up to a point
They tell a story all their own
But you must listen with your heart
To go beyond their dulcet tone.

Why don't we hear each other's pain?
How can we listen and not hear?
If you listen with your heart
The words of love ring true and clear.

When the purple shadows fall
Before the day has lost its light
You must listen with your heart
To hear God speak to you each night.

SMILES

I saw the sadness in your eyes
It could have been a trick of light;
For when I turned around again
You wore a smile that shone so bright.

I had not questioned what I saw
I had not gone that extra mile;
I had not seen your misery;
I had not looked beyond your smile.

I heard your voice catch on a sigh
You were embarrassed by the slip.
You coughed to try to pass it off
But sadness had you in its grip.

I had no right to question you,
I didn't want to try to pry.
You need to get it off your chest;
I hope you'll tell me by-and-by.

We all need someone in our life
To help us through our trial by fire,
The telling cuts our cares in half;
Our problems then don't seem so dire.

You need to trust the ones you love
With everything that's in your heart.

You may not get this chance again '
Ere circumstances make you part.

I might have thought your shiny smile
Revealed a life that's free of care,
But that's before I saw your eyes
And knew that you had grieved your share.

It's taken me a lot of years
Of seeing life, to be so wise;
To know the smile that's on your lips
Is not reflected in your eyes.

THE PEOPLE INSIDE

Who are these people that I see?
What are these aspects that I view?
They all come out from time to time;
They seem to live inside of you.

Your family sees a side of you
That no one else will ever see.
They think they know you best of all;
On that, you'll find, they all agree.

But family only sees the side
That you feel safe in showing them;
They see the rough cut of your stone;
They cannot see that you're the gem.

Your friends see yet another side,
They glimpse in you dramatic flair.
You tell them secrets of the heart,
But just those parts you want to share.

The public sees you at your best;
Your mask is firmly put in place.
You smile at them and woo them all;
They never really see your face.

These different people that I see
The ones that sit upon your shelves

Conflicted in their daily lives-
Your inner and your outer selves.

Take all these pieces of yourself
And mold them with a sculpting knife;
The ones that live inside of you
Must come together in this life.

Get rid of all your other selves
There's no more need to play a role;
If you need help to merge them all,
The God within can make you whole.

I WANT MY DADDY

Daddy's sick, Daddy's tired,
He's not in the mood for fun.
He's been working very hard,
He has no time for his son.

Daddy's working in the den,
Mom and I can't talk to him.
We have news I want to share:
Today I learned how to swim.

Mommy tried to interrupt,
Daddy looked up with a frown;
His work is more important
Than the fact I didn't drown.

When I cry out for his love,
Daddy pats me on the head.
"Be a good boy," he tells me;
"Brush your teeth and go to bed."

I've learned to walk on silent feet;
Daddy doesn't like the noise.
When I suck my thumb at night,
He says I'm not like other boys.

I try so hard to behave,
To obey his every rule;

I wonder if he'll love me more
When I'm old enough for school.

I once went to Daddy's office
And I climbed up in his chair;
I pretended to be him,
Because I knew he wasn't there.

I held his phone up to my ear
I got some gum stuck in my hair.
His papers scattered everywhere;
I quickly jumped down from his chair.

There was no rest for me that night;
My Daddy was so mad at me.
He kept me up and in a chair
He yelled all night; I couldn't flee.

I used to want to be like him,
Talking nightly on the phone;
But now I've come to realize
That he has a heart of stone.

When I grow up and have some kids,
I'll let them talk and have some fun.
No matter how they misbehave,
They'll still feel loved when I am done.

INVISIBLE WALLS

Why do you build those invisible walls-
To keep yourself in, or to keep us out?
We reach out to touch you and you withdraw
We tell you we love you, but you're in doubt.

What would it take for those walls to come down?
When will you trust us enough to be real?
Why do you keep us at such an arm's length?
When will you tell us what you really feel?

We talk about nothing and you feel safe;
The deep issues stay behind those high walls.
We know that you feel alone and afraid;
Please let us help you; we won't let you fall.

You've lived a life thinking that you're alone;
In your darkest hour, no one would come.
You've hidden behind those invisible walls
Shutting us out with the sound of your drum.

You don't ask for help because you can't bear
To know for all time that you might be right.
When you need us the most, you shut us out;
Your world is so dark; you've turned out the light.

You scream silently, "Please help me, please help.
I want to be loved. I'm lonely; I'm good.

I'm trying to reach out to let you in;
I'm tired of being misunderstood."

Take down those walls that have set you apart
Open the door of your self-imposed jail
Those invisible walls must be torn down
We'll be there to help you; you will not fail.

DID YOU HEAR THE NEWS?

Ann's shoes are scuffed;
Jim's head is bald.
Have you heard the latest dirt?
Bob left his wife for his mistress.
How could he leave with that flirt?

John lost his job and pension, too;
He had to file for bankruptcy;
He stands in unemployment lines;
I'm just glad it isn't me.

Those kids were beaten to a pulp.
Did you know that no one came?
The court date is three months from now;
Then, we'll find out who's to blame.

Did you hear Beth got her tubes tied
While her guy was out of town?
When he hears what she has done,
I don't want to be around.

Will raped a girl; they let him off;
His parents are too well-known;
They sealed the records from the trial-
Said the case was overblown.

Ted put his mother in a home
And told her he would visit soon
But now he says he can't go there
Because she's crazy as a loon.

Let's do lunch; I'll call you next week.
Did you see the sales today?
There's no more room on my charge card;
I'll borrow more if it's OK.

This kind of talk is very safe
It doesn't catch us unaware
We don't discuss what's in our hearts;
It never gets too close to bear.

It also takes no depth of thought
To talk about another's woes
Our minds shut down and words pour forth
And like the river, overflows.

Our words are sent out in the air
Like arrows pointed at one's heart
You'll never know the damage done;
So stop the words before they start.

THE SOUND OF SILENCE

The sound of silence fills the air
You use it as a punishment.
The house is quiet months on end;
The hurt you cause just isn't fair.

Your wife creeps by in silent tears
Emotions run too high to talk.
She can't express the rage she feels;
Her words are locked inside her fears.

Your daughter tries to placate you
She tries to be the perfect child.
Her stomach twists around in knots;
She doesn't know what she can do.

Your son runs wild; he is so mad
You quell his chatter with a look.
In his frustration to be heard
He tries his hardest to be bad.

In no more than a power play
You wield your silence like a club.
It doesn't matter whom you hurt
As long as you can get your way.

You'll never realize what's at stake
As bit by bit you've lost them all.

Their love for you has disappeared;
They've had as much as they can take.

When winter comes and skies turn gray
And everyone has gone away,
With no one left to tyrannize,
You'll sit in silence day by day.

THE DATING SCENE

You brush your hair a hundred strokes
Your makeup is perfection
Your shoes are laid out end to end
From your immense collection.

The latest styles are on your back
You have sophistication;
You're looking forward to tonight
With great anticipation.

He rings the bell; he's right on time
You don't like what he's wearing.
He talks to you about his day
But you're not even hearing.

The restaurant is not at all
What you had been expecting;
Although you're really quite upset
There's no point in objecting.

He starts to look around the room
To see what he's been missing
He spies a couple that he knows;
They're holding hands and kissing.

You start to tell him of your day;
He listens with just half an ear.

You see him scoping out the room
More interested to see who's there.

Neither one cares for the other
Yet you both expect a call;
When you see it's not forthcoming
You'll complain to one and all.

How can you find your heart's desire
When both of you are callow?
What conversations can you have
When both of you are shallow?

Look beyond the outer layer
Of the person that you see;
Connecting with each other's soul-
Loving for eternity.

NOT GOOD ENOUGH

Rejection is an ugly word
It corrodes your very soul;
No matter what successes come
You never feel completely whole.

Your mother loves your brother, Mike
Your father loves your sister, Sue;
You've always had this niggling feeling-
No one's there who just loves you.

Your school days passed by in a blur
From sandbox to your senior prom
"Please notice me," you seemed to say
"I feel just like a Peeping Tom."

You're on the outside, looking in;
No one knows that you exist.
If you should vanish from this earth
You can't be sure if you'll be missed.

An invitation went to all
They didn't think to send you one.
They danced until the crack of dawn;
You were excluded from the fun.

You lost your job; you stay in bed
You're too depressed to face the day.

The Classifieds have nothing new-
They'll hire you for dinky pay.

Your love affair has just gone south
She left you for another guy
You've been evicted for no rent
You're on the streets, left high and dry.

You're told your attitude must change;
You have been getting awfully rude.
Rejection does that kind of thing-
It puts you in a rotten mood.

Approval comes once in awhile,
You cannot count on it for long.
You'll never please the world at large;
You're just the singer, not the song.

You must live life on your own terms
No one else is in your skin.
Don't let rejection get you down;
Make your own rules and play to win.

THE LISTENING TREE

He sat on a branch of the tree
Complaining that life wasn't good.
He knew he should make changes now,
And said that he would if he could.

"I'm not a good listener," he said.
"It's quite a bad habit, I guess."
"You must fix it soon," said the tree;
"Your life is becoming a mess."

"Oh, that just isn't nice to say,
But it's fast becoming a fact.
You've taken my comfort away
And you're sadly lacking in tact."

The tree shuddered, and dropped a branch;
They'd had this discussion before.
It talked itself green in the face
And just couldn't take anymore.

"I give you advice when you ask;
We repeat the same things each day.
Why do you keep coming to me
If you won't follow what I say?"

"I never remember our talks;
I'm sorry my mind seems to drift.

You must have the patience of Job;
Your listening ear is a gift."

"My branches and leaves are dropping
From the many talks that we've had;
You never recall what I've said;
You don't even know that it's bad."

"I'm sorry, I'm sorry, I am;
I cannot help being this way.
I've always had trouble listening;
I'll pay more attention today."

The tree began to answer him,
But saw him jump down to the ground,
And when it looked around for him,
The man was nowhere to be found.

In sheer frustration, the tree shook;
Its leaves and branches tumbled down.
The man had talked its branches off;
The tree stood bare, its color brown.

A year went by before he came;
He called out to his Listening Tree.
But silence met his cries for help;
There was no answer to his plea.

He wept into his handkerchief
Because his tree was gone for good;

He said he would have listened more
If he had known and understood.

The Listening Tree looked on and sighed,
Its branches still upon the ground.
Its talk had ceased a year ago
And now it stood without a sound.

It wondered if the man had learned
That listening takes a special skill
You have to want to hear someone;
You have to keep your mind so still.

You have to listen to the words
And listen to the silence, too.
For listening is another way
Of someone showing love for you.

YOU THINK IT'S COMING TO YOU!

Entitlement is in the air
The world owes you a living.
You think that it should all be yours
But you won't do the giving.

You treat the masses with disdain;
You shove ahead of them in line.
You tell them that you're late for work
And still you show up half past nine.

Your colleagues wait for you to come;
Your attitude is very poor.
Your sloppy work is standard fare
At five o'clock, you're out the door.

Your clients wait for you to call;
They've hired you to do some work.
You listen to their messages;
They do not see you smile and smirk.

You break your promises each day
They can't depend on you at all.
You make a date and don't show up
Not even canceling with a call.

Your spending has gone off the charts
Your credit cards have reached the max;
You're buried under all your debts-
Now you can't pay your income tax.

You turn your nose up in the air
At those less fortunate than you.
You'd sell your mother for a song
To be among the privileged few.

You take from others what's not yours
It's so much easier that way.
It matters not how hard they've worked;
You've never learned about fair play.

You use the people that you meet
To help you get the things you crave,
Discarding them when you are through-
We can't be friends; I'm not that brave.

You have not earned your place in life;
You've let too many people down.
Your boorishness is out of hand;
You wear your rudeness like a crown.

The only value that is ours
Is how we treat our fellow man.
Our reputation's all we have;
We have to do the best we can.

The Golden Rule is not so hard
When we walk in each other's shoes.
Consideration is the key;
Divine law is the path we choose.

THE GREEN-EYED MONSTER

The green-eyed monster gets no rest
She always envies what you have.
It doesn't matter what it is,
Because she's sure you have the best.

If you are smart, she envies you
She doesn't try to use her brain.
She makes your answers fit her needs
It gives her that much less to do.

If you have friends, she wants them, too
She doesn't try to make her own;
Awareness doesn't come to her
She just keeps trying to be you.

Her jealousy eats at her soul
She hides it so that you don't see.
She compliments you to your face;
Resentment burns like fiery coal.

She doesn't see your misery
And if she sees it, doesn't care;
She wants what you have, good or bad,
Her jealousy's a mystery.

Why would a person crave the bad?
I thought she'd only want the good

But then I realized what's at stake;
She's only wanted what you've had.

We had this conversation once;
I told you of her jealousy.
I said she wanted to be you;
You laughed, and this was your response-

"I offered her my wordly wares;
It didn't seem to satisfy.
She says she wants to just be me
And then she won't have any cares.

"I find it hard for me to be
The kind of person that I am;
I can't believe that anyone
Would ever covet being me."

I told you not to take offense,
You can't control another's yen.
Don't try to find the catalyst;
A jealous nature makes no sense.

Just hide your goods from prying eyes
And only share them with close friends.
Don't tempt a jealous person's greed;
The green-eyed monster makes you wise.

SEPARATE LIVES

We seem to lead such separate lives
We used to care what each one did
We used to touch each other's soul;
The link we shared seems to have slid.

I listen to your life unfold
I want to tell you about mine
But you're so caught up with your own;
Your interest withers on the vine.

I know you want to care for me;
You didn't mean to turn away.
I try to tell you how I feel
The words won't come; I cannot say.

We sit there in our private worlds
We're each engrossed in our own thoughts.
It's doubtful if you'll ever want
The answers to the questions sought.

It saddens me that we have come
So far and yet we've lost so much;
Our yesterdays spent on the phone-
And now we barely keep in touch.

I look around and plainly see
The same thing happening everywhere

What is the matter with the world
That we no longer seem to care?

I look at people moving lips
The other one pretends to hear;
Nodding heads and vacant faces
Only listening with half an ear.

Our interests ranged beyond ourselves
We spoke of things from A to Z
And now the things that interest us
Are when we speak of "me, me, me!"

I try to find the link we lost
We need to care and touch again
We had so much in times gone past
I can't forget what we had then.

Let's find the bond we used to share
Let's teach our nation how to care
Let's find the bond that links mankind
Uniting people everywhere.

We have a chance to show our love
To make another soul feel good.
By showing interest in their lives
We join the ranks of brotherhood.

WHERE HAVE ALL OUR NEIGHBORS GONE?

The neighbors who looked after us
The ones we didn't know were there,
Protected us from unseen harm;
I look around and they're not here.
Where have all our neighbors gone?

We all grew up and moved away
We didn't know what we had lost
We spread our wings and left the nest;
Our freedom came at too much cost.

We're older now and not as wise.
Our neighbors now don't seem to care;
Our children go out in the streets
With none concerned how they must fare.
Where have all our neighbors gone?

I miss the neighborhood we had
Where all of us felt safe at night
Our neighbors all looked after us
We never felt far from their sight.
Where have all our neighbors gone?

A neighborhood is not a block;
It's more than just a street with trees.

It's more than schools, and stores, and banks;
It's more than a community.

A neighborhood's a tapestry
Of peoples's lives lived out each day;
Of nursing people when they're sick,
Of watching them at work and play.

It's helping them when they're laid off
When corporations must downsize;
It's sharing what you have with them
And listening to their silent cries.

It's watching out for latchkey kids
And letting them know that you care.
When both their parents have to work
It's kind of hard for them to bear.

A neighbor is the first to know
When pain is cutting like a knife.
A neighbor is the first to know
Important things about your life.

No matter how you try to hide
Your sorrows from your neighbors' eyes,
Don't waste your time; it does no good;
They see more than you realize.

When you must leave your neighborhood
You may not be up to the task.

You'll pack up all your memories;
You'll look around and then you'll ask,
"Where have all our neighbors gone?"

MR. BUSY EXECUTIVE

Hey, big shot, in your pinstripe suit;
Don't let success go to your head.
You're gone from home so frequently
Another man is in your bed.

You work long hours at your job
Neglecting children and your wife;
There's such a thing as balancing
Your family and your corporate life.

What happened to your common goals,
The ones that both of you once shared?
Don't you remember what they were?
The risks you took, the things you dared?

It's good to be tops in your job
But don't forget how you got there
You didn't get there by yourself
It took the help from everywhere.

Your parents paid your way through school;
They didn't have a dime to spare.
Now you're so busy with your work,
You don't take time to show you care.

Your wife worked hard to pay the bills
She worked two jobs from dawn till night;

She made sure that you dressed the part
That put you in the corporate light.

The sacrifices that were made
To get you where you are today
Were made by others, not by you;
The easy life just came your way.

For all the help that you've received
You'd think you'd show some gratitude.
You'd think you would acknowledge them;
Instead you cop an attitude.

Hey, Mr. Busy Executive
With the leather attaché case;
You have no time for your wife and kids;
Every day is a corporate race.

Your family wouldn't mind your hours;
They've always been your greatest fans.
If you'll include them in your life,
They'll be supportive of your plans.

If you will listen when they speak,
If you will make that first small start;
You'll see that they don't want your life;
They want a corner of your heart.

A life of balance is the key;
Consider this your wake-up call:

When work and family come together
You really can attain it all.

SH, DON'T TELL ANYONE

Don't tell the others what I said;
They'll think that I'm the one to blame.
I never know what's important;
To me all secrets are the same.

I don't know how to share myself,
I don't know what to talk about.
I cannot talk about my life;
The spoken word will not come out.

My heart has felt encased in ice;
I'm isolated by my fear;
My loneliness is paramount;
I'm ruled by secrets year by year.

My parents tell me not to tell
The things that go on in our house,
And so I've learned from childhood on
To be as quiet as a mouse.

I see my mother doing things
That she says not to tell my dad.
If he finds out what she has done
She knows he will be very mad.

My father tells me not to tell
That Grandpa is a closet drunk;

But everyone knows that he drinks
Whenever he gets in a funk.

I saw my father on the street,
His arm around his girlfriend's waist.
He told me not to say a thing;
It hurts to see that he's not chaste.

My sister creeps out late at night
To meet her boyfriend at a bar.
She's much too young to run around
With her unemployed Lochinvar.

My brother asks me not to tell
Our parents that he's smoking pot.
I'm sworn to secrecy again;
My stomach twists another knot.

I can't distinguish right from wrong;
I don't know which secrets to keep.
I feel so guilty if I tell;
I often feel I'm in too deep.

I have no value of my own,
So, secrets are my stock in trade.
By knowing all their dirty deeds,
It makes me feel I've made the grade.

It's second nature to me now
To say, "don't tell another soul;"

It boosts my self-esteem a notch
When others see me in this role.

The sad thing is I have no life;
I never know what's safe to tell.
When everything must be hush-hush
It makes my life a living hell.

I'd like it if, for just one day,
I could be free of secrecy.
I wonder what it would be like
To be the me that's really free.

LET'S TALK ABOUT ME

Whenever we're together
It's always, "me, my, mine."
If I never spoke about me
That would really suit you fine.

What is the matter with you
That you don't seem to care?
What is friendship all about
If you don't want to share?

I'm tired of this one-way street;
That's not how friends should be.
I'm tired of talking about you;
Now, let's talk about me.

I start to tell you of my life;
You've changed the subject twice.
What happened to courtesy?
What you did just wasn't nice.

I try to talk about the things
That won't bore you to tears,
But you're just waiting for your turn
As soon as I switch gears.

That doesn't make me feel too good;
I don't like what I see.

It's not a balanced friendship
If we can't talk about me.

The last time we were together
You didn't come up for air.
You never once asked how I was-
You didn't seem to care.

You tried to catch me up to date;
I tried to do the same.
But you seemed so distracted
And glad when parting came.

We can't continue in this vein;
That's not the way a friend should be.
We've talked about you enough-
Now, let's talk about me.

THROUGH THE EYES OF A CHILD

"Our Daddy always falls down drunk;
Our life with him has been pure hell."
"Hush, child, you mustn't say those things;
He isn't drunk; he's just not well."

"I don't know what is going on;
I'm six years old and not too wise.
I see my father lying there;
I fear because he cannot rise."

"Don't worry your poor head like that;
Our father just has had a spell.
He isn't drunk and he's not hurt;
He tripped against a chair and fell."

"You're seventeen; you'll soon be gone;
I don't know why you've stayed this long.
Don't tell me that he isn't drunk;
It always happens; I'm not wrong."

When Mommy drinks I just pretend;
I know I'm not supposed to talk.
She says she'll pick me up from school;
But when she drinks, I know I'll walk.

I try to be responsible;
It's hard within my six-year range.
I don't have fun; I don't know how;
I also can't adapt to change.

My brother, Jim, is ten years old;
These kinds of things roll off his back.
He hears our parents arguing
And makes a sandwich for a snack.

My sister, Lil, is now with child;
She turned fifteen a month ago.
She can't continue to live here,
Because no one's supposed to know.

When Karen leaves, she must take Lil;
The two of them will soon be gone.
There won't be money for the move;
They'll have to live with Uncle Ron.

I know I can't bring friends from school;
I never know what I will find.
I try to be invisible;
They yell and scream and act unkind.

My parents pull at me each day;
I can't show partiality.
I'm in this box; I can't get out;
I'm losing my identity.

I've learned that I can never talk,
And now I know that I can't trust.
I'm also learning not to feel;
I'm only doing what I must.

YESTERDAYS

I can't remember what we talked about;
We always seemed to have so much to say.
We'd part, and then we'd call with something new;
And now we sit in silence every day.

The world is bigger than the two of us;
We used to have an interest in it all;
We used to love to meet life's challenges;
The obstacles we faced were not too tall.

Remember all the arguments we had
About the way the country should be run?
Intensity ran high at fever-pitch,
Debating everything under the sun.

We got our highs from talking politics;
We volunteered in our community.
We carried placards when we fought a cause;
Sometimes not checking its validity.

We weren't cynical in times gone past;
We didn't know the meaning of defeat.
We even fought for justice in the courts;
We couldn't know the hurdles that we'd meet.

Perhaps we were naïve in our approach;
We thought that good would triumph over bad.

We hadn't yet seen life's inequities;
I'm sad to say I wish we never had.

Our years were marked by innocence of youth;
We only saw tomorrow, not our past.
We squeezed a thousand years into an hour;
We lived each day as though it was our last.

Our yesterdays flew by with dizzying speed;
I wish I could have trapped them in a jar.
I wonder where the years have disappeared;
They seem so near, and yet they seem so far.

It makes no sense to wish we had them back;
We're not the same inside that we were then.
I know we've changed so much in years gone by,
And yet I can't remember where or when.

If I could make a wish that comes to pass,
I'd like the passion that we used to share.
It animated everything we did,
Enriching both our lives beyond compare.

I wish I had the blazing zest of youth
And had not let our life just slip away.
There isn't much today that interests me;
I'm lost in memories of yesterday.

WHERE ARE YOU?

I never knew you were depressed
Or that you hated the rat race.
You didn't even say good-bye;
They say you left without a trace.

Where are you now? I'm wondering,
You didn't even leave a note.
You left your car and briefcase, too;
You didn't even take your coat.

Where have you gone?
Where are you now?
You emptied out our bank account.
The children cry themselves to sleep;
Their misery is paramount.

How could you just walk out on us?
How could we not know you were sad?
How could we not communicate?
How could I think we're all you had?

Our children think that they're to blame
For driving you from your own home,
And I feel guilty for our fight
That must have made you want to roam.

Where are you now?
Are you all right?
Are you getting enough to eat?
I think about you every day
And wonder if we'll ever meet.

We're too ashamed to tell our friends
That you ran off and left us here,
Without a care; without a cent
In this unstable atmosphere.

I blame myself; I should have seen
That I could never make you stay.
I can't remember if you said
That you would someday go away.

Our daughter walks around the house,
She thinks that this is all her fault.
Our younger son thinks he's not loved;
Our older son rules by default.

Detectives have searched everywhere
They think you left us in the night.
They do not think you disappeared;
They think you're hiding in plain sight.

Why would you want to leave our home?
So many questions crowd my mind.

I had not noticed your despair;
I can't believe I was so blind.

I wish that we had talked much more;
We used to talk all through the night.
I'm sorry that so much has changed;
I wish that I could make it right.

I want the life we had before;
I do not want to live alone.
I'm so afraid to face the day
When all the children will be grown.

I've never stood alone before;
I do not know if I can now.
It seems too hard for me to learn;
There's no one here to teach me how.

Where are you now?
Where have you gone?
I cannot face another day.
How had things gotten out of hand?
How could I know you wouldn't stay?

I pray for you each night in bed;
I hope your cares have left your brow.
I wish you all the best in life
And wonder where you are right now.

I also hope that someday soon
The rest of us will be all right.
I must make plans for all of us
So that our future will be bright.

So go, my love, enjoy your flight
The rest of us will all get by.
I will not wonder where you are;
I do not want an alibi.

I'm putting up our house for sale
We've all decided to move on.
But still the questions swirl around:
Where are you now?
Where have you gone?

THE TOUCH OF LOVE

You stiffen up when you are hugged;
Did no one hold you as a child?
Did no one sing a lullaby
To keep your cries from going wild?

Did no one kiss your little face
And tell you that you're loved so much?
And rocked you till you fell asleep
To soothing love felt in a touch?

The anger that you feel inside
The pain that always shadows you
Might not be there if you had felt
The loving touch of just a few.

The isolation that you feel,
Emotions you take care to hide;
When insecurities abound,
It makes you feel less loved inside.

There's no emotion on your face;
You act as though you've never cried.
And yet you have this empty hole
That can't be filled or satisfied.

You don't reach out; you cannot touch;
Discomfort oozes from your pores.

You squirm when someone touches you
We can't get through your concrete doors.

When we reach out and see you flinch
And not know what to say or do,
It's plain to see that you don't know
A touch is meant to comfort you.

When we touch you and you withdraw
The cold seeps in around our heart;
You can't imagine how it feels
To be so near, yet far apart.

Do you not feel the love we have?
Do you not want the bonding, too?
The signals that you send are mixed;
We're so confused; we have no clue.

Your words and actions never mesh;
You draw us close, but then you shove.
We wonder how it would have been
Had you once felt the touch of love.

I'VE HAD DESSERT; I'M DONE

Your selfishness astounds us all;
You may not like our point of view.
Your grasping nature's hard to take;
We wouldn't want to be like you.

You take from everyone you can;
It doesn't matter who they are.
And then you drop them in a flash
When they can't get you very far.

You make a meal of other's work;
You feast on all that they allow;
You take your fill and then you leave;
"I've Had dessert; can I go now?"

You show no interest in their lives
Until they start to drift away.
But if you want some more from them
You're nice until you know they'll stay.

It doesn't matter how they feel;
You squeeze the life from everyone;
You take until they're all wrung out;
You've had dessert and now you're done.

You're like a leech who just hangs on;
You suck the blood out of your friends;

They're left devoid of energy;
You take so much; it never ends.

You only care about yourself;
You have no use for anyone.
Your attitude has always been:
"I've had dessert; I'm done."

IT'S TIME TO SAY GOOD-BYE

It's been awhile that things went wrong;
It doesn't even matter why;
You only know that it won't work
And that it's time to say good-bye.

You gave your all; it didn't help;
You can't endure another lie.
There's nothing more that you can do,
And now it's time to say good-bye.

The blaming could go on and on
While accusations reach the sky;
There's naught to gain by staying on;
It's better if you say good-bye.

The disconnection that you've felt
Bespoke a parting that was nigh;
When it's more painful to remain,
You know it's time to say good-bye.

Relationships cannot be forced.
There's just so much that you can try;
And then you have to have the sense
To know when you should say good-bye.

There's nothing left of what you had;
If you don't leave, your soul will die.

When bad outweighs the good you had,
You know it's time to say good-bye.

Your bags are packed; the lights are off,
The well of love will soon be dry.
So close the door and don't look back;
The time has come to say good-bye.

APPENDIX

The Face in the Mirror

When I was growing up, one of the expressions that was popular in my day was, "Handsome is, as handsome does." We all knew that it wasn't enough to look beautiful or handsome; our actions had to match the face we presented to the world.

In one way, we took more care with our appearance than we do today, e.g., a woman wouldn't leave the house without the obligatory hat and gloves and a man wouldn't go to work in anything less formal than a suit and tie, but we all knew that it was more important to be good than to be beautiful or handsome.

Nowadays, we don't take the same amount of care with our appearance; we throw on a pair of jeans and T-shirt to go to the grocery store or even to go to work in companies that have an informal dress code, but the emphasis is no longer on the importance of being good.

In those days, we knew more about our neighbors and they knew more about us. We did more than just wave hello when we passed them in the street; we actually stopped to talk to them. If someone needed help, we tried to make ourselves available to them, and we all drew comfort in the thought that the next time, it could be us who needed their help.

Perhaps that kind of interest in one's neighbors is still alive and well in the small towns that dot our countryside, but it's almost unheard of in the metropolitan areas. Today, we're afraid to open our door to strangers or stop to help someone whose car has broken down on the highway because of all the horror stories we've heard about people getting murdered, robbed, or raped while trying to help someone.

With the advent of television, these horror stories are now brought into our living room on a daily basis. I think it's dehumanized us to a certain extent. Perhaps because we see so many atrocities on the nightly news, we don't personalize other people's problems; we don't think, "There but for the Grace of God, go I" and so we seem to distance ourselves from getting involved in anything unpleasant.

In the old days, people seemed to turn to God more often than they do now, both publicly and privately, in good times and in times of despair. Nowadays, the houses of worship fill up during the week only during a national crisis. That isn't to say that they were full during the week years ago, but it was more customary to take time to pray when it wasn't a national crisis or a religious holiday.

Perhaps people have gotten too jaded or too sophisticated to embrace a living God at the center of their lives during their quiet times, their times of aloneness, and only remember to do so, when it's a group effort and everyone can take notice of their devoutness.

We come into this world alone and we will leave it alone. At the end of a lifetime, we are left with memories of how our life has been lived. We stand in judgment of ourselves because no one knows us better than we know ourselves; while others may make excuses for some of our actions, we, alone, are privy to the motivations, thoughts, and emotions, that caused us to act in a certain way.

Therefore, since we are the only ones who can judge us accurately, it is important for us to live in accordance with our higher self; it is crucial for us to like the person we see in the mirror.

Don't Let Love Slip Away

Many people have no fear about taking physical risks, but they become almost paralyzed at the thought of taking emotional risks. They don't like to tell their partner "I love you" unless they know those words are going to be repeated back to them.

They don't like to tell anyone that they are in emotional pain and they're hurting, because they're afraid that it's going to be seen as a weakness and will be used against them, if not during that discussion, then at a later date. They often feel that it's easier to pretend that nothing is bothering them than to put their feelings on the line.

When people speak of intimacy, they often think of it in terms of the closeness that one feels while making love. While intimacy during sex is important, it's not the most essential factor.

The highest form of intimacy is mainly the ability to be able to tell someone your deepest, darkest thoughts and secrets and know that you can have honest discussions about them without fear of them being used against you in an argument. It is the ability to express your feelings without fear of retaliation, be it done overtly or covertly, and to know that what you say to each other in private will never be repeated to anyone else or used to win an argument.

In the absence of deep communication about feelings, relationships have a way of drifting apart. Invisible walls begin to go up around the two of them and separate them, making it impossible to talk about anything more than trivia.

Most people don't notice the early signs that their relationship is slipping away; it is usually a very gradual process that has its roots in a lack of trust, secrecy, and the inability to talk about the things that really matter to them. When they start talking about trivial matters all the time, instead of occasionally, or combined with more meaningful conversations, it's only a matter of time before the relationship completely disintegrates.

The Listening Heart

There is a psychic connection that flows between people who care about one another. This is the kind of relationship where we find one person finishing the sentences of the other person, where oftentimes one of them starts to say something at the exact moment that the other one was thinking it; the kind of person who sees behind the words, who listens with the heart instead of just the ears. This is listening and caring at its best. It doesn't take the place of verbal communication; it just places it at a higher level and promotes a greater depth of honesty and intimacy.

Listening is an art. First, you have to be genuinely interested in the other person, and then, you have to really care what the other person is saying. You might be able to get away with having your mind wander during some of these conversations, but the person who is talking to you, will usually feel the loss of your attention; it feels like the discussion is being short-circuited and you can actually feel the disconnection taking place.

When this lack of interest in your partner's life becomes the norm rather than the exception, your partner is made to feel unimportant and boring and relationships start to deteriorate.

Smiles

This poem is about how we accept things at face value without questioning what we see. Many people seem to prefer the type of "feel good" relationships that don't inconvenience them. They are so wrapped up in themselves, that they don't look beyond the superficial. They don't want to take the time, or make the effort, to connect with people on a deeper level.

When you don't want to listen to someone else's problems, it's easier if you can accept that person's smile at face value and smile back at them in that same "feels good" sort of way. By ignoring the pain that's in their eyes, you don't have to have an uncomfortable conversation about their troubles.

It seems these days that people do more to cover their unhappiness because they don't have the feeling that anyone really cares about them. And family and friends find it easier to go along with the pretense because then they don't have to become involved.

Much of the depression that people have today is due to the fact that they feel isolated and have no one to talk to about the things that matter. The people who care deeply about their relationships, know that the eyes are the windows of the soul, and when their loved one smiles at them, they look to see if their smile reaches their eyes.

The People Inside

A well-integrated person has the ability to temper what he says to match other people's personalities or set of circumstances, without changing the person he is, and without people perceiving him differently. He is the same person when he is at work or at home, with colleagues, friends, or strangers.

One of the saddest commentaries on our way of life is the number of people who are afraid to show their real self. I always hear comments like, "If you knew the real me, you wouldn't like me," or they will say, "I'm only this funny or this intelligent when I'm with you; I'm not this way with other people."

Why aren't they this way with other people? We all have our own dragons to slay and none of us is perfect, so why are people afraid to show their imperfect self to all the other imperfect people in the world? Why are they so sure that no one would like them if they knew the truth about them?

We might know someone, but no matter how well we think we know them, we fall far short of the mark of really knowing them. People usually show us only a small side of themselves and often they act one way with one person and another way with someone else. The rest they keep hidden.

There's an old saying that you don't know someone until you've lived with them, but I think that even when you live with someone, you still don't know them very well. You might know how they will react under certain circumstances, you might know their moods, or their favorite colors and foods; you might know their reading and entertainment preferences, but you can't possibly know their real self if they never show it.

I think family members know you least of all because they are so accustomed to seeing you every day that they don't bother to look below the surface to see who you really are. And, of course, colleagues, friends, and strangers only see a minuscule part of you because they aren't with you enough to see much more.

I Want My Daddy

Chances are, if you ask parents whether they consider themselves good parents, the majority of them will say yes. For many of them, providing a roof over their children's head, and feeding and clothing them, constitutes being a good parent. They often fail to notice that they are neglecting their children's emotional needs.

When a parent is too busy or too preoccupied to listen to his child's stories and to be interested in his day-to-day life, the child often feels that he isn't loved and that he needs to work harder for that love. He doesn't see that there might be other reasons for this benign neglect; he just sees it as his own failing.

A person's enthusiasm for sharing an experience is tamped down when he hears words like, "I'm tired." "I have a headache." "I'm coming down with a cold," and it's even worse if he is constantly hearing "I brought home some work that I have to do tonight because I have a busy day tomorrow." These words have the effect of ice water being poured over the one who has been bubbling over with excitement, who couldn't wait to share his news. It stops him cold because he knows that the other person is not going to be in the mood to hear his news.

Many people utter the words, "I'm tired" or "I'm not feeling well" out of habit; it's so automatic that there is no thought involved. They don't even realize that these words, when used frequently, create a barrier to intimacy because even when they are physically present in the room, they are emotionally absent. It's even worse when they barricade themselves behind telephone calls and office work; it's as if there is an invisible ring-pass-not between them and the other person.

If adults can feel this barrier, how much worse is it for small children who see their parents as gods, and who want so desperately to please them and be loved by them?

Invisible Walls

Although the invisible walls in this poem can be used to describe many people, during my years of counseling others, the one pattern that plays out over and over in the victims of physical and sexual abuse, is a sense of loneliness, isolation, and helplessness, especially when it starts at a young age.

These people are afraid to ask for help because they think that no one will come to their rescue. They go through life believing that they are totally and irrevocably alone; that in their darkest hour no one will come, and then they make that belief come true by asking no one TO come. They retreat behind their invisible walls, shutting out the world when they need people the most.

These wounded people have great difficulty with intimacy; they don't fully trust anyone and have difficulty sharing their feelings. They don't like to ask for help, believing that they can't count on anyone but themselves; they, therefore, try to do everything for themselves, by themselves, effectively shutting out the very people who love them and want to help them.

Did You Hear the News?

The gossip mill seems to be a national pastime. Whether it's employees standing around a water cooler talking about their bosses or coworkers, people talking on the phone about their friends or relatives, or people congregating at the local watering hole or at parties, gossip seems to be alive and well.

There is an air about it that goes beyond the realm of caring about the person under discussion. There is an insatiable curiosity for information that has nothing to do with a genuine interest in the person or a desire to help him. It's often a case of one-upmanship, "I know something you don't." It makes the bearer of the news feel important for being the first to know and the first to share it with others, or if he can't be the first, then it's his way of feeling as though he is one of the crowd, an accepted member.

Gossip is also a way of preventing intimacy, of deflecting personal questions so that people can't get too close to you. If you're talking about other people's problems, there is less likelihood that the focus will be on probing your secrets that you don't want to share. Some people have minimal conversational skills and if they couldn't talk about other people, they would have nothing to talk about.

Then there are those who either don't have the mental capacity to talk about deeper subjects or who are too lazy to do so; either way, gossip eliminates that problem because it's far easier to repeat stories than to think about interesting things to talk about. There's also an old saying, "small minds discuss people, average minds discuss things, and great minds discuss ideas."

Gossip can be destructive. People's reputations can be destroyed overnight, feelings can be hurt, and relationships can end, all on the basis of something that has been said directly, or hinted at, or unintentionally overheard. While it has been said that if you don't want to hear anything bad being said about you, you shouldn't eavesdrop, it can also be said that when you hear your name being mentioned, the most common reaction is to listen to what's being said about you.

Because you can't control the things that are being said about you, you are always at the mercy of those who have an ax to grind and those malicious people who get their kicks from maligning people. There's no way to fight an unseen enemy and that's precisely what you're up against when you are the subject of gossip and you don't even know what's being said about you.

And even if you do find out what people are saying, you can't go around to every single person and correct their misperception. As I said, gossip can be very destructive. If you talk about others, you can expect them to talk about you, and if you tell someone a juicy tidbit about someone else, the person you're talking to will rightly assume that you will talk about him to someone else. If you don't want to be the subject of gossip, don't participate in the telling of it; it always comes back to haunt you.

The Sound of Silence

There are all kinds of silences: the comfortable ones, the contented ones, the scared ones, the overly emotional silences where the person is too choked up to talk, and the silences used as punishment.

The person who said, "Speech is silver but silence is golden," never had to endure silence when it was being used as a punishment. If anything can destroy the fabric of a relationship, it's when people communicate their anger by a wall of silence.

Some people slam cabinets and doors or throw things to emphasize their rage, but refuse to speak, while others use lethal looks to nail someone to the cross. Still, others can look through you as if you don't exist, or they avoid you like the plague, while others talk around you as if you aren't there by telling a family member, "ask your mother when dinner is going to be ready" or "ask your father if he is going to be home this weekend" when they are standing no more than three feet away from each other.

No matter which way it is done, the end results are always painful and more anger and resentment are being added to the growing list of offenses stockpiled against you. I have watched this wall of silence being used in every strata of society and in every type of situation.

It doesn't matter whether it's being used in the home, at work, in the classroom, or anywhere else, it is one of the most effective tools a person can use to show his anger or to make the point that what you're doing, is not acceptable to him. It is also the most damaging tool a person can use and one that can fracture a relationship beyond redemption.

The Dating Scene

In the old days, dating was much simpler than it is today. It wasn't better, but it was simpler. Men and women were introduced to each other by a friend or family member or they met at their religious social functions, and because there was always someone to account to, they obeyed the social mores.

Women didn't go to bars and they didn't get picked up . . . at least the "nice" women didn't. Women didn't call men; they sat by the phone waiting to be asked out on a date and there were even rules about that. A man had to ask a woman out by Wednesday for a Saturday night date or she told him she was busy. More often than not, she had to settle for one of the men who wanted to marry her, since society didn't allow her to pursue the man she wanted to marry.

Fast forward to today's dating scene. Men and women meet each other in singles bars and anywhere else that single people congregate. They meet online in chat rooms, message boards, and dating sites. Women have much more latitude today; they call men for dates, pay for their dinners, and aren't expected to be a virgin on their wedding night. But with the changing roles comes a myriad of problems.

Nowadays, since friends and relatives haven't introduced couples to each other, there seem to be fewer restraints. There is more date rape, excessive drinking, and other behaviors that would have been unacceptable in the old days.

People have become much more superficial; they seem to be searching for something or someone better even while they are in the company of someone else.

I hear a lot of men say that the guys who get the gals are the ones who mistreat them. And then I hear the women say that they are looking for someone who treats them well. And, of course, I'm always hearing about people dating someone for their looks or money, and this is now on both sides of the gender line.

In the old days, men and women were looking for home and family; today, women are delaying marriage in favor of career, and by the time they are ready to settle down and start a family, there seems to be a shortage of available men who want the same thing.

Good communication has always been a complaint between the genders, but now there is the added problem of not knowing what they really want, and if they do know what they want, they don't necessarily know when they want to make that commitment.

Not Good Enough

I don't know anyone who hasn't experienced rejection in one form or another. It comes in all forms and it starts in early childhood from the parents to the siblings, to the kids in the sandbox.

Children can be unbelievably cruel to one another and can say the most hurtful things without realizing the consequences. Is it any wonder that one's defense mechanisms are firmly in place by the time a child enters the first grade? The adult mind can forgive the things that were said and done to him when he was young, but the child within him remembers every word and act and is still harboring those hurt feelings.

If you ever want to see how a child will turn out as an adult, watch him playing with other kids. Later in life he may learn how to mask his feelings but the child within him is still alive and well and reacting just the way he did on the playground.

One of the severest forms of rejection can be seen in the dating scene. People of all ages can be incredibly cruel in the way they decline a date. They can even be cruel in the way they refuse a dance. After being subjected to that kind of treatment and subjecting others to that kind of treatment, is it any wonder that people enter relationships with a lot of baggage? Is it any wonder that people are suspicious and wary and afraid of being hurt?

I've watched how people argue and handle anger. Some people will tell you that when they get angry, they blow up and then the anger is gone. That may be fine for them because they're able to get it out of their system, but it's not fine for the other person who is left feeling bruised, angry, and resentful but too afraid to say so.

When people yell at you in anger, they might not tell you that in their anger, they often say despicable things that can never be forgotten by the one who is being vilified. After it's over, the one who has hurled those mean and hateful words can apologize till the cows come home, but the damage has been done because those words will remain forever in the other person's mind.

Not too many couples can survive that kind of rejection in their relationship; this probably accounts for much of the hard feelings that are encountered in a divorce.

The Listening Tree

There are some people who are energy drains. They come to you with their problems but they are really not interested in hearing what you have to say. All they want is someone to listen to them, and anyone will do, although they would like you to believe otherwise.

These people make you feel as though you are the only one who has the answers to their problems, but in actuality, you find yourself talking to a stone wall because they aren't listening.

The scenario is always the same; they tell you their problems and you put a lot of thought and energy into giving them the best insights that you have, but they aren't really listening. No matter how often you have this discussion, these people don't try to change their situation nor do they try to solve their own problems. Each time you have this discussion, it's as if they are hearing your words for the first time, although the subjects don't vary.

This situation can be very addictive for both the complainer and the advisor because the complainer doesn't have to learn how to think for himself and the advisor keeps thinking that it's worth all the time and energy he's investing because the complainer is making progress.

The reality is that the advisor is wasting his time and energy because the complainer doesn't really appreciate the advisor's efforts, nor is he making permanent progress; it's only window dressing, smoke and mirrors, to keep the advisor hooked on wanting to focus his complete attention on the complainer. The complainer doesn't really want a solution to his problems because then he wouldn't have anything to complain about.

In the end, the advisor may realize that he's too tired to do his own work because he has been expending so much time and energy solving the complainer's problems. Although he may feel bad that he has to limit or stop dispensing advice to this person in order to be more productive in his own life, he will shortly come to realize a cardinal lesson: he's not indispensable, and it won't take long before his advice is being replaced by someone else's.

Another indisputable fact is that one listening ear is the same as another's because the complainer isn't looking for solutions; he's only looking for someone to focus his complete attention on him. With that in mind, he will always find someone to use as his psychic garbage pail.

You Think It's Coming to You!

There seems to be a pervasive attitude of entitlement in today's society; so many people expect everything to be handed to them on a silver platter. Their desires vastly exceed their needs, but they seem unwilling to work for what they want.

We have only to see children nagging their parents for what they want, and parents caving in to their demands because it's too stressful to argue with them, to see the kind of adults these children will become. I once heard a young man say that if he couldn't get what he wanted by working for it, he would steal it.

There's an old saying: "What you are at seven, you'll be at seventy." When children grow up, they leave their childhood toys behind. Why, then, don't they leave their childish attitudes behind, too? Why do we tolerate their "gimme" attitude in the workplace and in relationships, where their expectations are high and their efforts are minimal?

We have fostered a couple of generations of spoiled people who don't know how to treat their fellow man. They want to do half the work for twice the pay. They agree to do a job and then they don't show up or they do a poor job. Promises seem to mean nothing these days.

When I was growing up, I always heard that a person is only as good as his word. Today, parents promise children something, be it reward or punishment, and then don't follow through. These children grow up to become adults who make promises to employers, co-workers, family members, friends, clients, or creditors and then break their word as if it were of no importance.

Interestingly enough, I've heard some people who were being chastised for breaking their promise, try to defend themselves by saying that the other person is being anal, as if that were justification for breaking their word. And then we complain that the crime rate is up, pension funds have been embezzled, and spirituality is lacking in our society.

The Green-eyed Monster

If you have ever been jealous of someone or been the target of someone else's jealousy, then you know how distressing it can be. When we think of the mental and physical anguish that jealousy induces, we can understand why John Dryden described it as the jaundice of the soul; it truly does injure us more than the people we envy.

Although we often think of this character flaw in connection with romantic relationships, it just as often taints the relationships between siblings and friends.

Even strangers are not exempt when we realize how frequently people are jealous of those they have never met, e.g., celebrities, captains of industry, those who seem to have a life of ease or who are extremely successful in any area of their life.

Look at the tendency we have of trying to elevate those at the bottom, and when they reach the top, we try to topple them; it's as if we begrudge those who have succeeded beyond a certain point, when we are struggling with our own day-to-day challenges.

Most people experience the occasional twinge of jealousy when they perceive someone as having more than they, or they suspect someone of deliberately trying to deprive them of what they most desire.

A person's insecurities or fears can cause him to be jealous of someone who is more attractive or who has more financial success, social status, talent, etc.; they don't even have to want what the other person has; they just don't want that person to have it.

One of the classic jokes about jealousy is the one where a woman is walking along the beach and she finds a bottle and uncaps it, and out pops a genie who grants her three wishes for freeing him. Knowing that this woman has always been very jealous of her sister, the genie tells her that she can have anything her heart desires but there is a condition to her wishes: whatever she wishes for, her sister will get ten times more or better.

The woman wishes to be the most beautiful woman in the world and the genie warns her that her sister will be at least ten times more beautiful than she. The woman doesn't care because she will be living thousands of miles away from her sister and everyone she knows will see her as the most beautiful woman in the world. So, poof!! - she's the most beautiful woman in the world!

Then she wishes to be the richest woman in the world and the genie warns her that her sister will be at least ten times richer. The woman doesn't care because she is sure that her investments will increase in value more than forty times what she will pay for them, making her richer than her sister. So, poof!! - she's the richest woman in the world! For her third wish she tells the genie that she would like a mild heart attack.

But the reality of jealousy is not a joking matter; it is a destructive force that makes people behave in ways that alienates others and drives away the love they crave. Excessive insecurity, feelings of inadequacy, fear, anger, and anxiety, are the catalysts of jealousy that make everyone's life miserable.

If it were not such a common emotion, there wouldn't be so many books, plays, essays, and songs being written about the subject. William Shakespeare's character, Othello, is a classic example of how this emotion can be taken to the extreme when Othello kills his wife in a fit of angry jealousy for her supposed infidelity. In its less severe form it can just cause unwarranted unhappiness and severed relationships.

Separate Lives

It's sad to see people drifting apart. It starts out innocently enough; you're preoccupied with a situation and your mind starts to wander in the midst of a conversation.

You're sitting at the dinner table listening to the small talk going on around you and suddenly you're thinking about something else; the expression on your face remains the same and no one knows that while your body is present, mentally and emotionally, you have parted company. This separateness that one experiences, even when surrounded by other people, is so profound that it's as if each person is sitting at the table all alone.

The beginning of a relationship is an exciting time; there is so much to tell and so much to share that you run out of time before you run out of conversation. Because you are interested in everything about each other, you see yourself reflected in the other person's eyes, and this makes you feel prettier/handsomer, wittier, more intelligent, more charming, and more of everything.

Your old stories take on a new luster and they suddenly become more entertaining in the telling than ever before. You feel yourself becoming more interesting and you make your partner feel more interesting; it's as though each of you by yourself, is just an ordinary person, but when you are together, you become extraordinary.

As time passes, if they don't continue to invest a lot of time and energy into keeping their relationship alive, they start to lose interest in each other's lives. They no longer have a million and one things to discuss; they laugh less frequently, they give each other only the bullet points of their lives instead of sharing the rich tapestry of their experiences, and they no longer feel comfortable confiding in each other. The intimacy is gone and just the memories that bind them, remain.

When we look at the broader picture, we see the same lack of connectedness happening all around us. We hear of people starving, political prisoners being tortured, natural disasters that leave people homeless and in abject poverty, heinous crimes being committed, and we're only momentarily moved. We might donate money, food, and clothing, but after a short burst of altruism, the tendency is to let the problems of others fade into the background.

Only by a sustained interest in the lives of others, can one hope to understand the true nature of relationships, and to find the golden thread that links us to all humanity.

Where Have All Our Neighbors Gone?

A child's first external sense of security comes from his neighborhood. This is where his first friendships will be formed, where he will go to school, and where he will experience his first ideal of community.

It is in his neighborhood that he will learn that people can care about you and can be there when you need them, without being your friend or your relative. They do not have to share your values or your philosophy of life but you have a sense of protection, knowing that neighbors see each other come and go on a daily basis and, when there is a break in a pattern, a neighbor is usually the first to notice it and investigate it.

There are loosely defined boundaries in a neighborhood, ranging between the need for privacy and the need for friendship, between what you are willing to share of your personal life and your public persona.

Since a neighborhood is defined by the people living there, it must be expected that neighbors talk to each other, and about each other. Very little escapes their notice and while it can often feel stifling to know that your every action is being noted and commented on, it is also reassuring to know that when you are in trouble, it is your neighbors who are usually the first to come to your assistance.

If you are seen leaving your house every morning and then one morning you don't leave your house, one of your neighbors will probably knock at your door to see if you are all right. And while it can often feel restrictive, it can also be a comfort to know that someone cares about you.

In the days before the advent of dryers, neighbors talked to each other over the clotheslines while they were hanging their clothing out to dry. Nowadays, although society moves at a much faster pace, neighbors still manage to congregate at mailboxes, block parties, schools, bus stops, restaurants, houses of worship, libraries, street corners, shops, and community centers.

While a neighborhood is often seen as the sum of its parts, e.g., schools, stores, banks, houses of worship, etc., it is really more about the people who live there. It is a sense of people helping each other in times of need and celebrating with them in times of joy, but most of all, it is about the sense of belonging.

Mr. Busy Executive

People often lose sight of the important things in life once their goals have been achieved. They may start out as idealistic, wanting to make the world a better place, and somewhere along the way, their objectives change, they become more self-centered, and more materialistic.

When people marry young and finances are tight, the dreams of one may be sacrificed for the other if there is a long educational road ahead of them.

It starts out with the agreement that one of them will put his or her life on hold, working as many jobs as it takes to put the other through school, and then they will switch roles, and the other will go to school for their degree while being supported by their partner.

What happens in too many cases is that when it's their turn to get their degree, there are too many obstacles to surmount, e.g., responsibilities of raising a family, burdens of school loans, etc., and their dreams never come to fruition. As if that weren't bad enough, all too often, the one whose goals were achieved, suddenly decides they have outgrown their partner and divorces him or her, replacing the outmoded spouse with a shiny, new, trophy spouse. Sometimes this occurs after the person has become successful and sometimes it occurs right after graduation.

Success often comes with a high price tag. Instead of showing their family and friends appreciation for the emotional and financial support they received while climbing to the top of their career, they frequently neglect their greatest champions by taking them for granted, disregarding their needs, and being too busy to spend time with them.

The true measure of success comes not from how much money a person makes but from how it is interwoven into the fabric of one's life. A healthy bank account is only the means for paying one's bills; it is not the criterion of happiness or emotional freedom. For that to happen, a successful person must find a way to bring balance into his life.

Just as there is a separation of night from day, so must there be spaces between the need for companionship and the need for solitary moments, between speaking and silence, between praying and meditating, between listening and talking, between thought and action. There must also be a balance between work and play, pleasure and duty, sadness and joy, exercise and relaxation, giving and taking, saving and spending, and career and family.

It is the balance between mind, body, and spirit that ensures a person of a harmonious and fulfilling life, capable of maintaining one's health even under the most stressful situations; this, then, is the hallmark of a successful person. "

Sh, Don't Tell Anyone

Secrets can be empowering or disabling depending on the nature of the secrets and on the frequency with which a person is asked to withhold information. When a child is very young, the tendency is to share every thought and every impulse and he answers questions freely; communication is open and free-flowing.

As he grows older, he becomes more protective of his inner thoughts and feelings and often resents the questions of adults, seeing it as an invasion of his privacy. After so many years of seeing his parents as omniscient and omnipotent, there is a certain sense of power associated with keeping secrets from them.

When he grows older secrecy becomes part of the bonding process in forming friendships, e.g., pinkie swearing, clubs that have secret passwords and handshakes, and pricking fingers and then touching each other's droplet of blood while swearing promises of eternal friendship, loyalty, and secrecy.

These are the normal aspects of secrecy in children and it would be endearing if it stopped there. However, in many households, secrecy becomes a way of life, protecting the atypical behavior of a family member, e.g., an alcoholic parent, a family member who is on drugs, or who is abusing another family member physically, sexually, or mentally, or one who has been committing incest, etc. These children have a very hard time knowing the difference between keeping an innocent secret for a friend or having secrecy become a damaging way of life.

Up to a certain point, secrets are a way of forming bonds, but carried to extreme, they become unhealthy barriers that prevent intimacy. It is next to impossible to have an open and loving relationship with a person who hides a large part of himself from you. Rather than seeing the hidden part as something mysterious and alluring, it becomes a source of discontent to know that an important element is missing from your relationship.

On the one hand, a person may get a boost to his ego every time someone asks him to keep a secret, but on the other hand, he often finds himself isolated from his peers. When a person can't remember, or can't distinguish, what is supposed to be confidential, his communication becomes guarded and limited to issues that don't involve the lives of others.

This veil of secrecy frequently gets in the way of having normal relationships because the individual may be so afraid of revealing someone's secret, that he only feels safe when he talks about impersonal matters. In essence, he becomes a prisoner of his own making, never feeling free to be himself.

Let's Talk About Me

I think the unhappiest people in the world are the ones who are self-absorbed. They are so wrapped up in themselves and their problems that they tend to isolate themselves from the rest of humanity. It's as if nothing else exists for them outside of their own little world.

When you talk about the things that interest you, their eyes glaze over and it's patently obvious that they are not listening to anything you're saying and that they find your conversation boring. After awhile, it becomes very difficult to share confidences with these people or to have them be part of your life because they are not really interested in anything about you. They can talk endlessly about themselves, but they have neither the interest nor the patience to listen to you talk about anything that doesn't focus on them.

These are the kind of people who listen impatiently to what you're saying . . . for a very short time . . . and as soon as you take a breath, they rush right in and change the subject to something more interesting, namely themselves. It's difficult to have a relationship with someone who is only concerned with having a relationship with himself.

Through the Eyes of a Child

I think one of the deepest forms of rejection a child can face comes from having an alcoholic parent or, in many cases, two alcoholic parents. Some alcoholics become maudlin, incoherent, or jovial, but more often they become mean-spirited and violent.

The children often feel invisible, unloved, and unprotected. They learn that it is safer not to trust anyone, not to talk about personal things, not to feel anything, and not to depend on anyone. They often grow up not knowing what normal behavior is, and not even being able to identify their feelings. They have a well-developed denial system about their feelings and their perception of what is happening in the home.

The rule here is survival. While many of these characteristics can be seen in children who come from dysfunctional families, they are a classic pattern in children of alcoholic parents.

A new report* from Substance Abuse and Mental Health Services (SAMHSA) shows that 7.5 million children in the past year under the age of 18 have lived with a parent who abuses alcohol. According to this study, an estimated 6.1 million of these children live with two parents; either one or both are abusing alcohol. The 1.4 million of those children, who remain, live with a single-parent who abuses alcohol. 1.1 million of these children lived with a single mother and 0.3 million children lived with a single father.

Data from the National Health Interview Survey, 2010

Overall, 51% of adults aged 18 years and over were current regular drinkers, 14% were current infrequent drinkers, 6% were former regular drinkers, 8% were former infrequent drinkers, and 21% were lifetime abstainers

Fifty-nine percent of men were current regular drinkers compared with 43% of women. Men were also more likely to be former regular drinkers than women. Women were more likely to be current or former infrequent drinkers or lifetime abstainers than men.

Recent data from the National Institutes of Health, 2012

Reports 15% of the people living in the United States are considered "problem drinkers." Of this 15%, 5%-10% of the males and 3%-5% of the females could be labeled as alcoholics. Another study found that approximately 30% of people in the U.S. report experiencing an alcohol disorder at one point in their lifetime. Researchers from the University of California in San Diego have found that the lifetime risk of alcohol-use disorders for men is greater than 20%. They share that there is a risk of around 15% for alcohol abuse and 10% risk for alcohol dependence.

More than three million teenagers are alcoholics.

Researchers from the Harvard School of Public Health say about one-half of college students are under age 21, and regular use and abuse of alcohol is part of many students' environments.

How prevalent is alcohol abuse?

Alcohol is the number one abused substance by teenagers in the United States. Its prevalence in this age group is quite staggering. According to the National Center on Addiction and Substance Abuse - Columbia University, "underage drinkers account for 11.4% of all the alcohol consumed in the United States."

Some studies done by NIAAA (National Institute on Alcohol Abuse and Alcoholism) have shown the following:

Prevalence in 8th graders:

51.7% have tried alcohol

43.1% have had an alcoholic drink in the past year

25.1% have been drunk

15.2% have had 1 or more binge drinking episodes

Prevalence in 10th graders:

70.6% have tried alcohol

63.7% have had an alcoholic drink in the past year

48.9% have been drunk

25.6% have had 1 or more binge drinking episodes

1.9% have been daily drinking for at least 1 month at some point in their lives

Prevalence in 12th graders:

80% have tried alcohol

73.8% have had an alcoholic drink in the past year

62.3% have been drunk

30.8% binge drank in the past 2 weeks

3.6% use alcohol daily

Children of alcoholics are often at the mercy of their parents' moods and unable to count on them for emotional support and, in many cases, to protect them from physical violence or verbal abuse. They can't even depend on them for consistency and predictability. They learn not to trust and not to confide in anyone because they are sure that no one will be there when they need help.

Because of the unpredictability of their parents to perform the simplest of things like remembering to pick them up after school, giving them lunch money, keeping a promise to take them somewhere, remembering their birthday or other important occasions, or being sober enough so they don't embarrass their children when they bring their friends home, these children learn that if they need something, they had better figure out how to get it for themselves because no help will be forthcoming from anyone else.

Communication is almost nonexistent. Children from alcoholic families are taught that they have to cover up the truth to strangers about what goes on in their home; they are apt to be very secretive, seldom talking about themselves or their families in a meaningful way.

They have been taught to pretend that everything is great about their home life and to preserve the deep, dark secrets of the living hell they have had to endure. They are often filled with anger, fear, and guilt, although they may not know how to identify those feelings or how to resolve them in a constructive way.

Yesterdays

I've always wondered why the passion we had in youth diminishes as we get older. Perhaps it's because in the innocence of youth we don't have the added burden of the layers of experience to weigh us down, or perhaps, as we age, our physical bodies slow us down and we're forced to set priorities on how we use our energy.

In youth, we see the years stretching out before us and we think we have forever; life hasn't had a chance to beat us down with interminable disappointments. We also have that sense of immortality, that feeling that we are indestructible, and there is an excitement and energy that infuses all our actions. We're young, idealistic, and more than ready to fight the good fight for all our myriad causes.

As we get older, we may still have an excitement and energy that infuses our lives, but it's more restrained and well-considered. Age makes it necessary to choose our battles carefully because we now have the wisdom to know that we can't fight vigorously on every front, nor do we have the energy to do so.

In the fullness of time, we pursue careers, get married, and have children; we have more at stake and more to lose. With added responsibilities, we become less adventurous, more cautious, and less willing to take risks. As the naïveté of youth gives way to disillusionment, the curiosity and idealism that marked our earlier years must, of necessity, become more tempered.

The sad part about the aging process is that we become complacent; we become more absorbed in our personal problems and less concerned about correcting the larger societal issues. As people get older and have had a chance to reflect on their lives, they often express regret for some of the things they have done. My regret would be more for the things I didn't do, rather than the things I have done.

Where Are You?

When a person's troubles seem insurmountable, there is often an overwhelming desire to run away and start over. They fantasize about chucking everything and just disappearing off the face of the earth. Fortunately, most people don't act out these fantasies.

However, thousands of people do go missing each year and unless a crime has been committed, law enforcement agencies usually don't get involved.

Historically, men have been the ones to leave home when they were discontented, while women felt obliged to make the best of it and stayed home to raise the children.

Over the past several decades, this trend has been reversed. Women are now leaving in larger numbers and, like their male counterparts, they leave voluntarily and without a trace.

There seems to be so much discontent in today's society and the unsettling thing about it is that it's kept inside and isn't discussed. Families live in the same house, see each other every day, talk about a million things, and have no idea what is going on in the minds and hearts of their loved ones. And then one fine day, one of them disappears into thin air and no one suspected that anything was wrong.

Some of the missing people who have been tracked down, or who have returned home voluntarily, tell some amazing stories. Most of them planned their disappearance very carefully, often, for many years in advance of their taking off.

Through the underground, they find ways to change their identity, obtain a new driver's license, get a new social security card, and open up a bank account wherever they plan to relocate so that when the time is right to leave, they can just vanish without anyone being able to trace them.

The reasons people leave home vary widely. Some are into so much debt, they cannot see any way out of their problems except to start over with a new identity. For others, there is the stress of having too much responsibility and/or trying to live up to everyone's expectations. Others leave because of family conflicts, abuse, depression, illness, problems at work, or unfulfilling careers. For most, it's the temptation to escape and get a second chance at life without having to resolve the problems they want to leave behind.

When a loved one disappears without an explanation, the family members who are left behind must deal with an incredible amount of guilt and insecurity. They wonder if they were the cause of the person's unhappiness and if there was anything they could have done to prevent him or her from leaving.

Their lives are indelibly affected; they question their own judgment and wonder how they could have thought they knew the other person so well, only to discover they didn't know that person at all.

They feel unloved, vulnerable, abandoned, betrayed, often financially insolvent, and they suffer losses of self-worth and self-confidence. These people will probably face a future of having difficulty establishing intimacy in their relationships because they will be afraid to love and afraid to trust.

The Touch of Love

It's a painful experience to hug someone who doesn't like being touched. When a hug is offered in friendship or solace and the recipient stiffens up in the embrace, it's awkward for the hugger and discomfiting for the huggee. The one being hugged is ill at ease at the contact, and the one who is offering consolation or a show of affection, feels rebuffed when the other person stands like a stone statue during the hug.

Many studies have been done showing not only the importance of being touched, but that it is critical for the development of a newborn. They have experimented with children in hospital nurseries where one group of infants were not picked up, and their needs were met in an impersonal way, and the other group of newborns were picked up, cuddled, rocked, sung to, and talked to.

It was found that the group of infants who were touched and caressed, thrived on it and the ones who were not touched, fared very poorly or were harmed by it. They have even found that some infants will die if they are not physically stimulated through touch.

When an infant is touched, it is his first sensory experience of being loved. It satisfies his emotional needs, and the sense of security that he feels, allows him to develop into a highly functional adult who is capable of having healthy relationships.

When an infant has been denied the loving touch of an adult, it is very hard for him to learn how to get his emotional needs met, and he has a great deal of difficulty moving from being self-absorbed to having the capacity to feel compassion for the needs of others. It is also a major deterrent to intimacy because it keeps the other person at a distance and sends the message not to get too close.

I've Had Dessert; I'm Done

Some people go way beyond the point of being selfish. These are the "users," the people who take and take and take, with no thought of giving back unless they think they may need you for something else. Most of them have learned how to get the most out of people without the ones who are being exploited even being aware that this is happening.

It may start out with a "user" asking you to do something small, e.g., check a document for mistakes or look up a piece of information; then it may go to the next level of asking you how you would phrase a paragraph, and before you realize what is happening, you are writing the paper for them and/or doing the research for them.

The "users" know how to sound grateful for everything you do for them and usually compliment you every step of the way to keep you motivated to do more for them.

More often than not, the "user" will thank you profusely in private but, in public, will pass your work off as his own not giving you the credit you deserve.

Occasionally, you will find a "user" who knows the value of public recognition; he doesn't really appreciate your efforts but he knows that if he lavishes praise on you in public, you will be highly motivated to continue to do his work for him.

One of the characteristics of a "user" is his ability to make you think you are being valued as a person or as a friend during the time your services are being used. Then, as soon as you have fulfilled your purpose and there is nothing else that you can offer, you are dropped like a hot potato. If there is a remote possibility that you will be needed in the future, the contact is at least minimally maintained, keeping you on tap, to ensure that you will be available the next time you are needed.

Most "users" don't really care about you unless it furthers their objectives. They often feign an interest in you and your concerns in order to get the most out of you. When they need you, they don't particularly care if you are exhausted or have too much on your plate; their needs come first. As long as you continue to serve a purpose in their lives, they will take great care to make you feel important but as soon as you stop being of use to them, you will find yourself discarded like yesterday's garbage.

It's Time to Say Good-bye

For a variety of reasons, people often stay in unhealthy relationships long beyond the point where they should have left. For those who believe in karma and reincarnation, these couples give the appearance of having overstayed their karmic welcome. For those who don't believe in it, it's akin to having stayed too long at the party and being the last one to leave.

Why do people stay in relationships that have stopped being enjoyable? For some it's the fear of starting over or parental or societal pressure. For others, it's not being able to face the reality that the only thing that sustains the relationship is memories of the past, and not the way they are relating to each other in the present. For still others, it's the fear of not being able to make it financially or emotionally, and for others, it's an addiction or a habit, or a reenactment of an abusive childhood.

For whatever reasons people stay in relationships that are no longer satisfying, when they finally do get the courage to walk out, they will have to deal with their unresolved feelings and memories for a long time to come.

Anger, hurt, disappointment, frustration, despair, regret, and sadness, are the most common emotions that one experiences at the end of a relationship. Some people say they are able to get on with their lives as soon as that door is closed. I seriously question that. The end of a relationship requires the processing of emotions and this is done very slowly, layer by layer.

Many times, a person thinks he has resolved all the issues that sabotaged the relationship only to find that years later, those same issues will crop up again in other relationships or in other areas of one's life. The resolution is to examine not only the relationship that just ended, but to examine one's self to see why you attracted that kind of person in the first place. It's also to see whether you've learned the lessons that that relationship provided.

There's never a perfect time to end a relationship, but when the bad outweighs the good, when everything you do isn't enough, that's the right time to go. Anger and hurt can exacerbate the problems, each one striking out to inflict emotional damage to the other. When people are gripped in the intensity of their anguish, it's better to leave the relationship while they are still capable of being civil to each other.

ABOUT THE AUTHOR

Connie H. Deutsch is an author, renowned consultant and spiritual advisor who has a keen understanding of human nature and is a natural problem-solver. She is known throughout the world for helping clients find workable solutions to problems that are often complex and systemic in nature and part of a corporation's culture or an individual's pattern of behavior.

Connie's depth of experience lends itself to both corporate consulting and individual counseling. Perhaps Connie is best known for her "homework" assignments which serve as virtual road maps for moving clients through problems into living solutions.

In addition to her consulting and counseling practice, Connie has hosted her own weekly radio show, is a regular contributor to the spiritual and personal growth website *Next Level Soul* (www.nextlevelsoul.com) and is one of the most downloaded guests ever on the popular *Next Level Soul with Alex Ferrari* podcast.

She has been a guest on numerous cable, radio shows, and podcasts around the country. She wrote a weekly advice column for sixteen years and has been has been invited to speak at universities around the world.

Visit her website at www.ConnieHDeutsch.com

next level SOUL™

Next Level Soul™ is a resource for spiritual seekers, and curious souls who are looking to find the deeper meaning in their lives. On NLS you will learn from some of the world's top spiritual and thought leaders. To help you on your spiritual path NLS publishes books, audiobooks, courses, weekly podcasts, and videos. We are here to help you on your life's journey and awaken your inner peace.

Next Level Soul™ founder, Alex Ferrari is a #1 best-selling author, speaker, entrepreneur, award-winning filmmaker, spiritual seeker and podcaster. His industry leading podcasts, the Webby award-nominated Indie Film Hustle, and Bulletproof Screenwriting have been downloaded over 11 million times to date. He has had the pleasure of speaking to icons like Oscar® Winner *Oliver Stone* and *Billy Crystal,* music legends like *Bruce Dickinson* (Iron Maiden) and *Moby* (Grammy® Award Winning Music Icon), actors like

Edward Burns (Saving Private Ryan) and *Eva Longoria* (Desperate Housewives), thought leaders like 2X Nobel Prize Nominee *Dr. Ervin Laszlo* and *Dr. Eben Alexander* (Proof of Heaven) and New York Times Best-Selling authors Dan Millman (The Way of the Peaceful Warrior) and Dr. Raymond Moody (Life After Life).

Throughout his life's journey Alex was always asking the big questions. Why are we here? Is this all there is? What is my soul's mission in this life? He developed NLS to help people around the world get closer to their own higher power; to look inward for the answers they are searching for.

The *Next Level Soul™ Podcast* was created to help answer those questions by having raw and inspiring conversations with some of the most fascinating and thought provoking souls on the planet today.

For more information on Next Level Soul:

Official Site: www.nextlevelsoul.com
Next Level Soul Podcast: www.nextlevelsoul.com/podcast
Next Level Soul Books: www.nextlevelsoul.com/books

THOUGHTS AND REFLECTIONS

I wanted to create a space for you to write down your thoughts and reflections after reading sections of the book. Think of this as your own personal addition to the book. Look inside yourself and write down what you are feeling right now. You will thank yourself in the future.

_____

_____

_____

_____

_____

_____

_____

_____

_____

_____

_____

_____

_____

www.ingramcontent.com/pod-product-compliance
Lightning Source LLC
LaVergne TN
LVHW011204080426
835508LV00007B/586